The Fiddlin' Workshop for Viola

Jeanine Orme

To access the online audio go to:
WWW.MELBAY.COM/30773MEB

WWW.MELBAY.COM

Introduction

This book was written to be used as a learning tool for student violists who want to play fiddle tunes. While it contains the same tunes in the same keys as the original *The Fiddlin' Workshop* and *The Fiddlin' Workshop for Cello*, many of the arrangements have been modified to make fingering for viola easier with minimal shifting. For some tunes, more than one version is presented. The tunes are written in the typical keys that most fiddlers use. The book presents easy tunes to learn the basics of bowing and style and progresses in difficulty with each tune.

Fiddle tunes can be played in many different ways and each fiddler has his or her own interpretation of how a tune should be played. This book provides practical fingerings and bowings for each tune, often with additional information or instruction. Fiddlers can add their own interpretation of slurs, bowing, ornamentation and rhythmic feel to develop their individual style.

About the Author

Jeanine Rabe Orme began playing the violin at age five and was fiddling by the time she was eight. During her youth she performed with the Utah Old Time Fiddlers and began entering fiddle contests. She competes regularly at the Weiser National Oldtime Fiddlers' Contest, as well as other state and local contests. She is a past Utah State Fiddle Champion and Oregon State Fiddle Contest Young Adult and Adult Division winner.

Her music was influenced significantly by the late Herman Johnson of Shawnee, Oklahoma. Mr. Johnson instructed her in Texas-style fiddling as well as in the swing fiddle style.

Jeanine has been teaching fiddle lessons for over 40 years and regularly teaches fiddle workshops and camps. She has also played fiddle, bluegrass and swing music with various bands in Utah and Oregon. Jeanine resides in Beaverton, Oregon and is the mother of three adult children.

Acknowledgements

Technical help with the audio tracks was provided by Jon Newton.

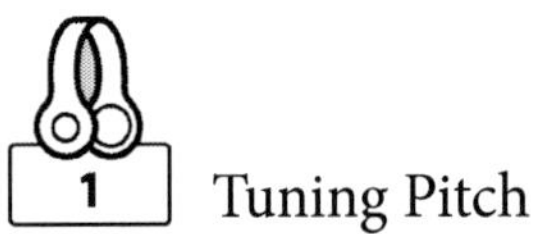

Tuning Pitch

Contents

Overview of Musical Symbols and Style

sl. **Slide the finger** - This marking indicates that a slide adds to the style of the song.

A **Section marking**

Grace note - Ornamental note with no value by itself. Slur quickly into the next note.

Triplet - Grouping of three notes played in the same time allotted to two notes of the same value.

D. C. al Fine - Return to the beginning and play until you see the word "*Fine*"

Double stop - two notes played at the same time.

Example: 0 4

4th finger and open string are played together.

Fingering - Finger numbers are indicated when correct fingering makes a difference in the ease of playing or adds to the style of the tune.

Shifting - A shift to third position is marked with correct fingering.

Guitar Chords - The guitar chords presented in this collection are basic and functional. Many variations or additional chords could be added.

Tips on Bowing

1) The wrist of the bow hand should be flexible, not stiff. Use more wrist movement, especially on passages that are fast.

2) In general start a new phrase with a down bow to accent the first beat.

3) Use a pattern of three-note slurs instead of two-note slurs. Your bow direction will not change if you add or take away a three-note slur.

Bowing Interpretation - The bowing style for this collection is based on a pattern of three note slurs. When you use a three note slur, the bow direction does not change. Each phrase usually begins on a down bow. This style of bowing will generally yield a smooth flow of notes.

Example 1 - Two-note slur pattern:

Example 2 - Three-note slur pattern:

Developing Swing Rhythm

Many fiddle tunes (including waltzes) should be played with an *implied* swing rhythm of the eighth notes. It is customary to write swing rhythm as "straight eighth" notes, but when "Swing rhythm" appears over the first measure, the pairs of 8th notes are played as triplet figures.

Swing rhythm

A swing rhythm is *approximated* in the quarter note with eighth-note pattern below:

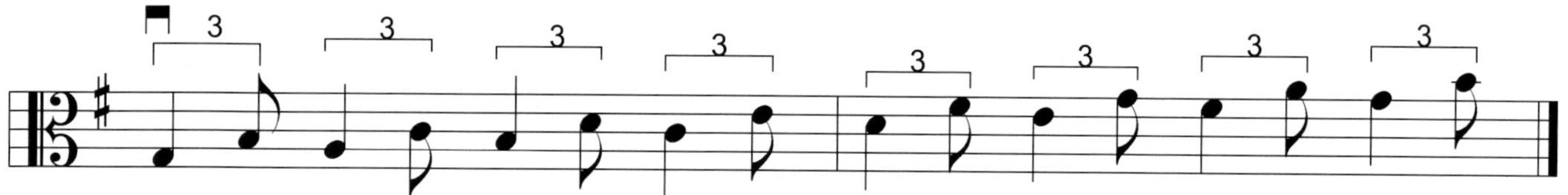

Scales and Key Signatures

The following major key signatures are used in this book:

C Major-lower octave

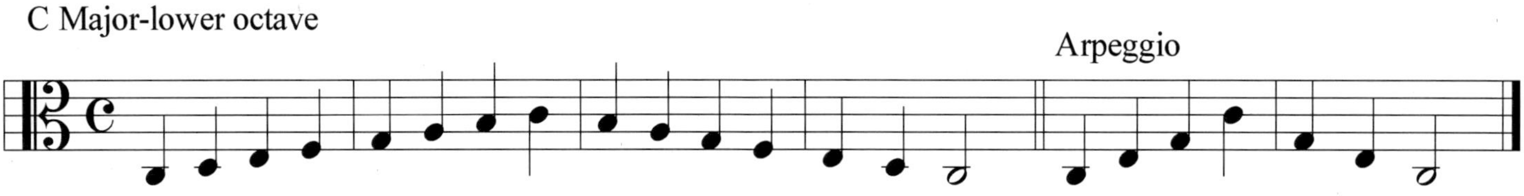

Arpeggio

C Major-higher octave

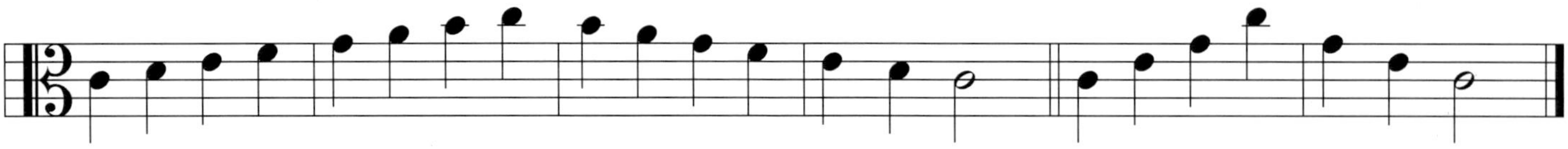

G Major

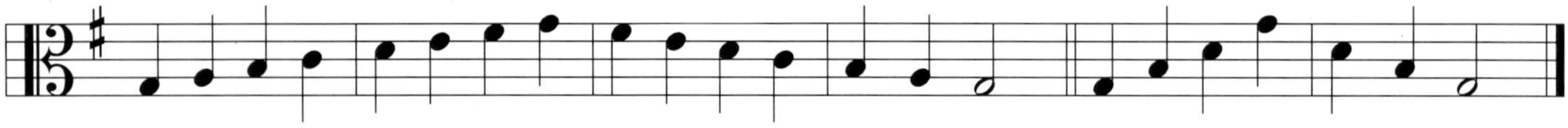

D Major-lower octave

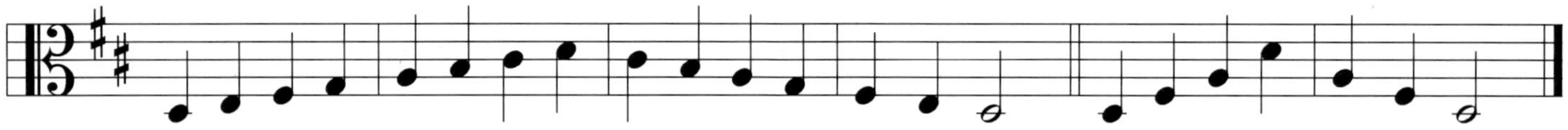

D Major-higher octave

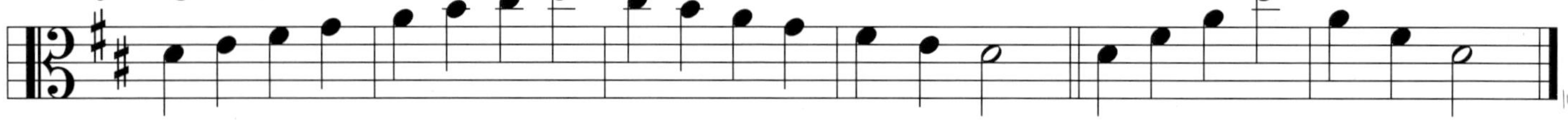

A Major

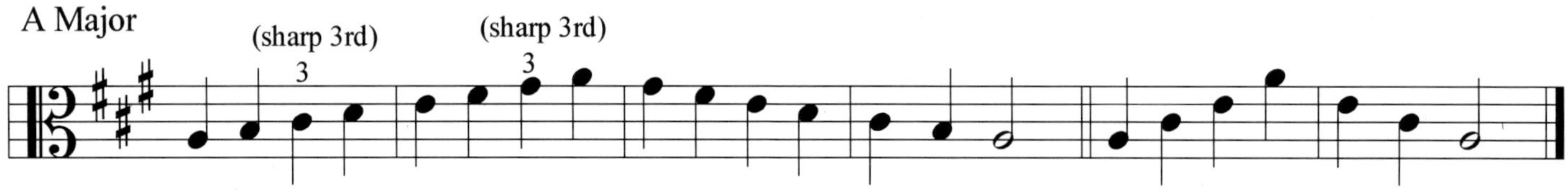

(sharp 3rd)
3
(sharp 3rd)
3

Introduction to Shifting: Shifting to Third Position

When a shift to a higher note is needed, shift the entire hand to the new location keeping the basic left-hand formation.

F Major

1
2
3
3
(shift up)
(shift down)

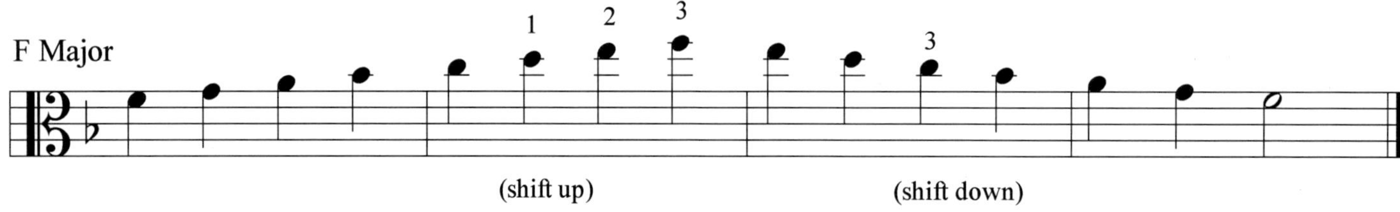

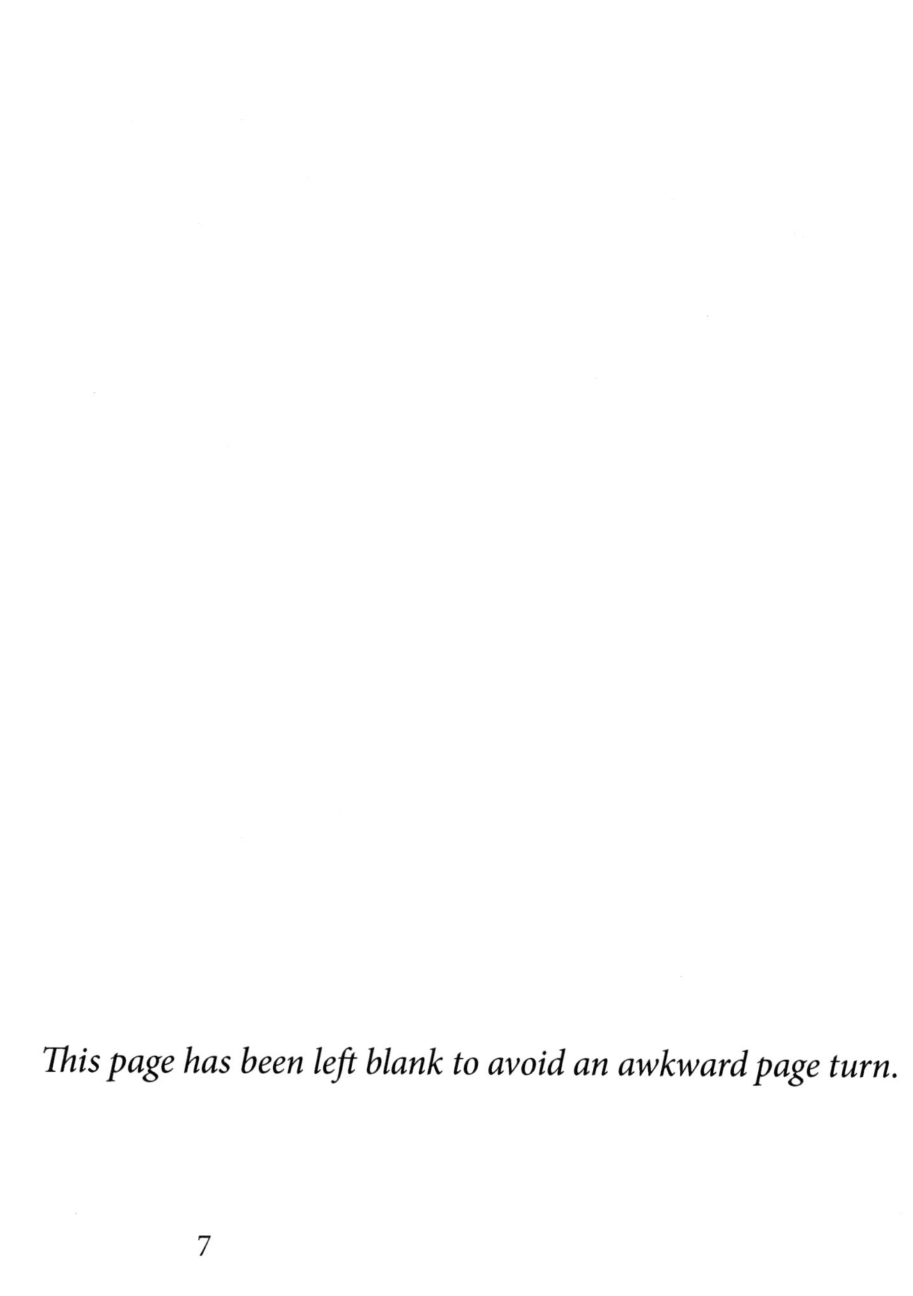

This page has been left blank to avoid an awkward page turn.

Soldier's Joy

Straight rhythm
Fast tempo

Traditional

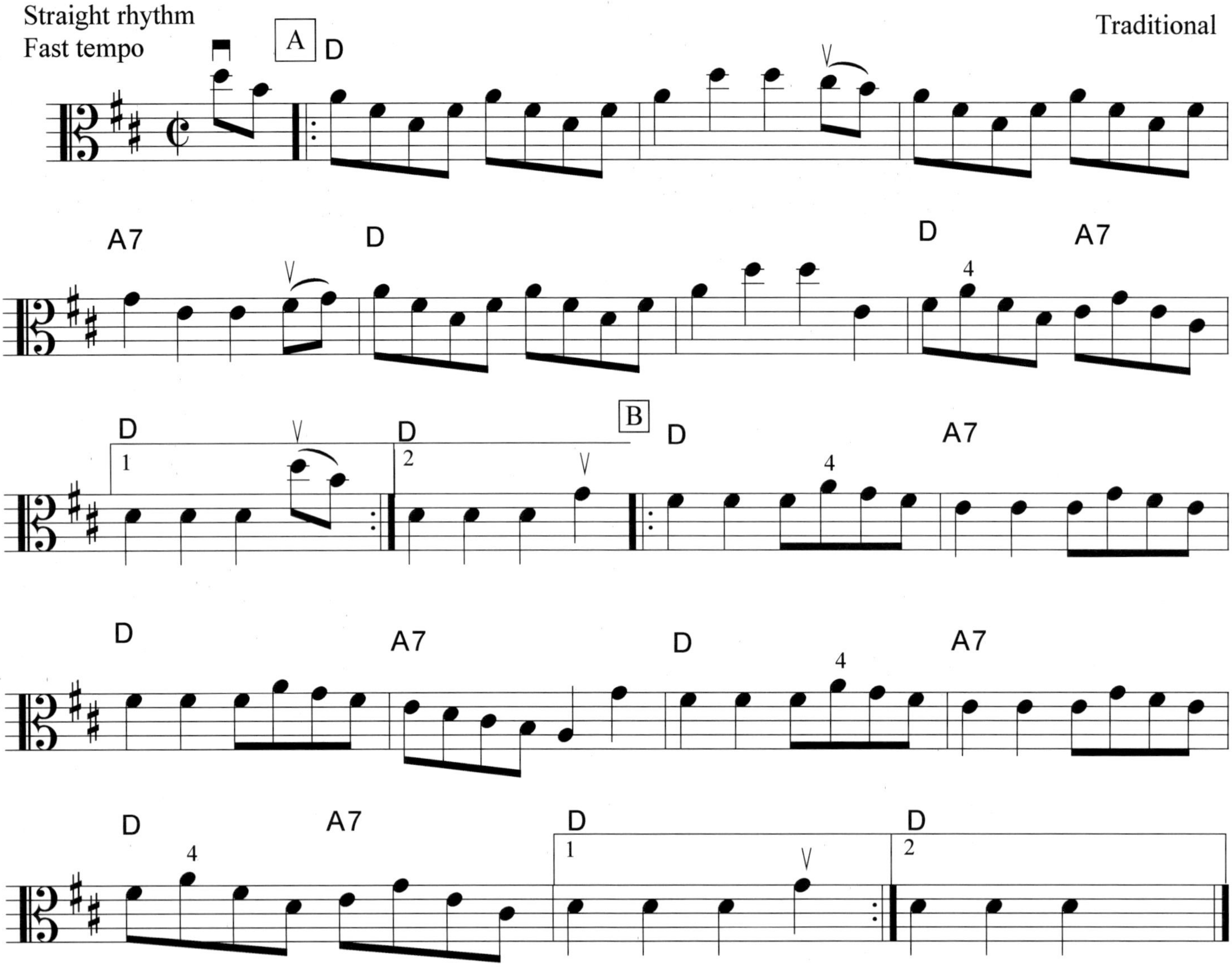

A D A7 D D A7 D D B D A7 D A7 D A7 D A7 D D

These variations can be used in place of the [B] section in "Soldier's Joy" to add variety. An example of using the variations can be heard on the audio track.

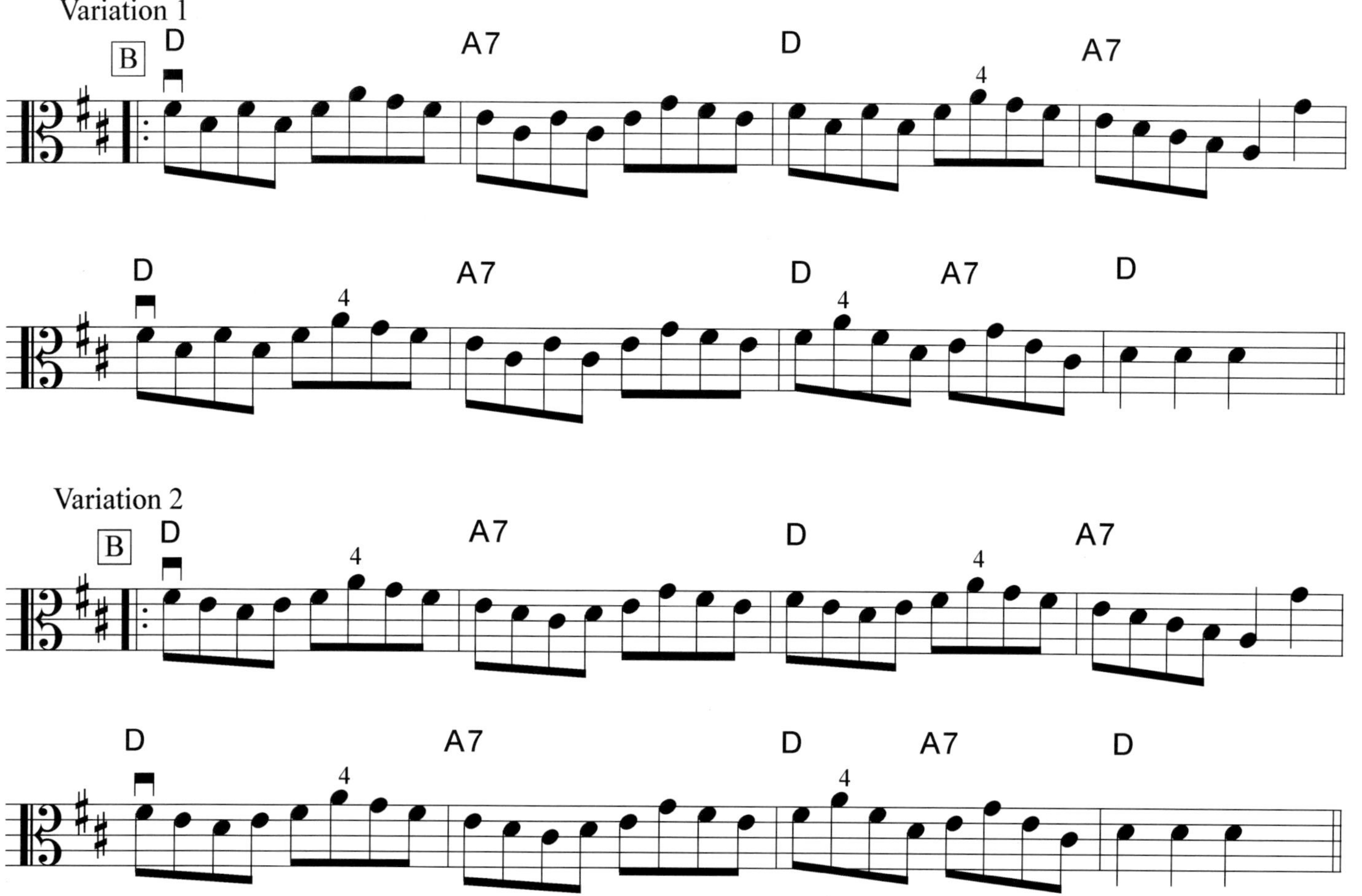

Arkansas Traveler

Straight rhythm
Fast tempo

"Arkansas Traveler" is a reel with a familiar melody.

Traditional

A D G A7 D A7

D G A7 D

A7 D 1 A7 D 2 B D 4 G D A7

D A7 D A7 D 4 G D A7

D A7 D 1 A7 D 2

Part [A] of this tune can be played an octave higher as follows:

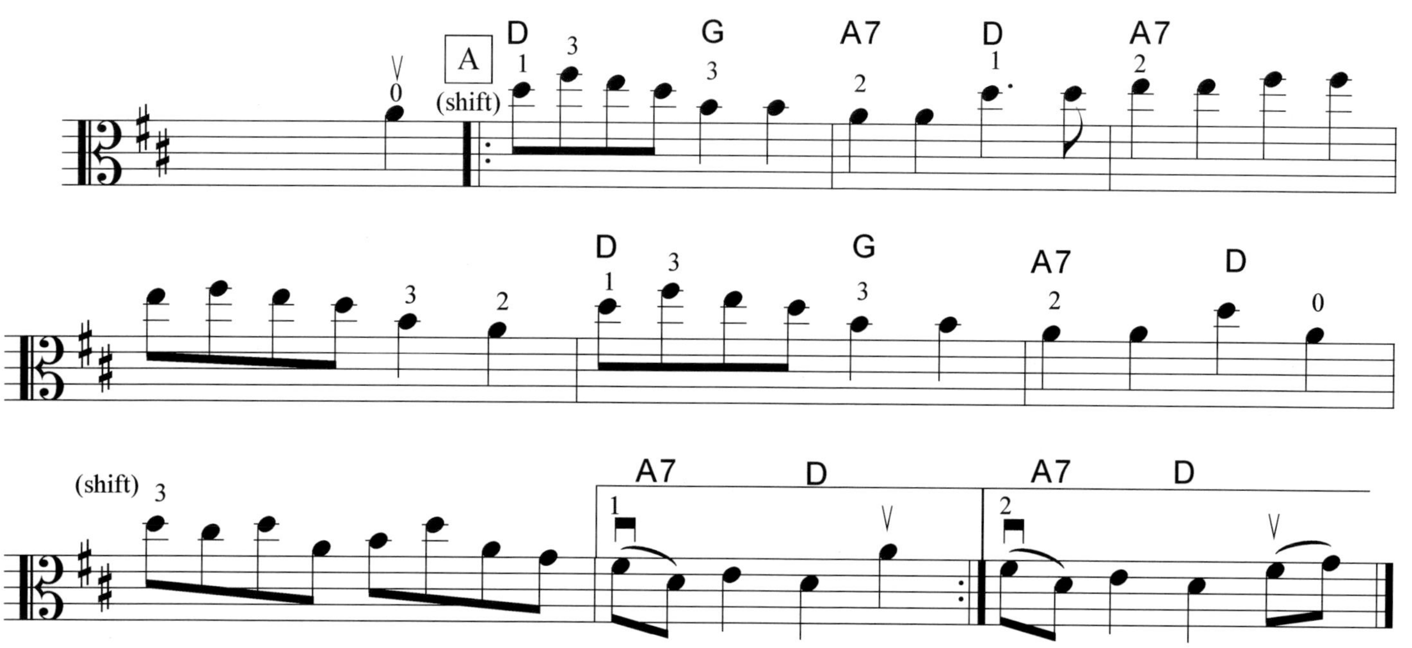

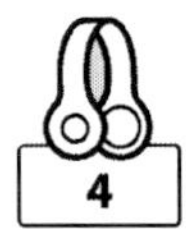

Devil's Dream

"Devil's Dream" is traditionally played in the key of A
but it can easily be played in the key of D as well.

Straight rhythm
Fast tempo

Traditional

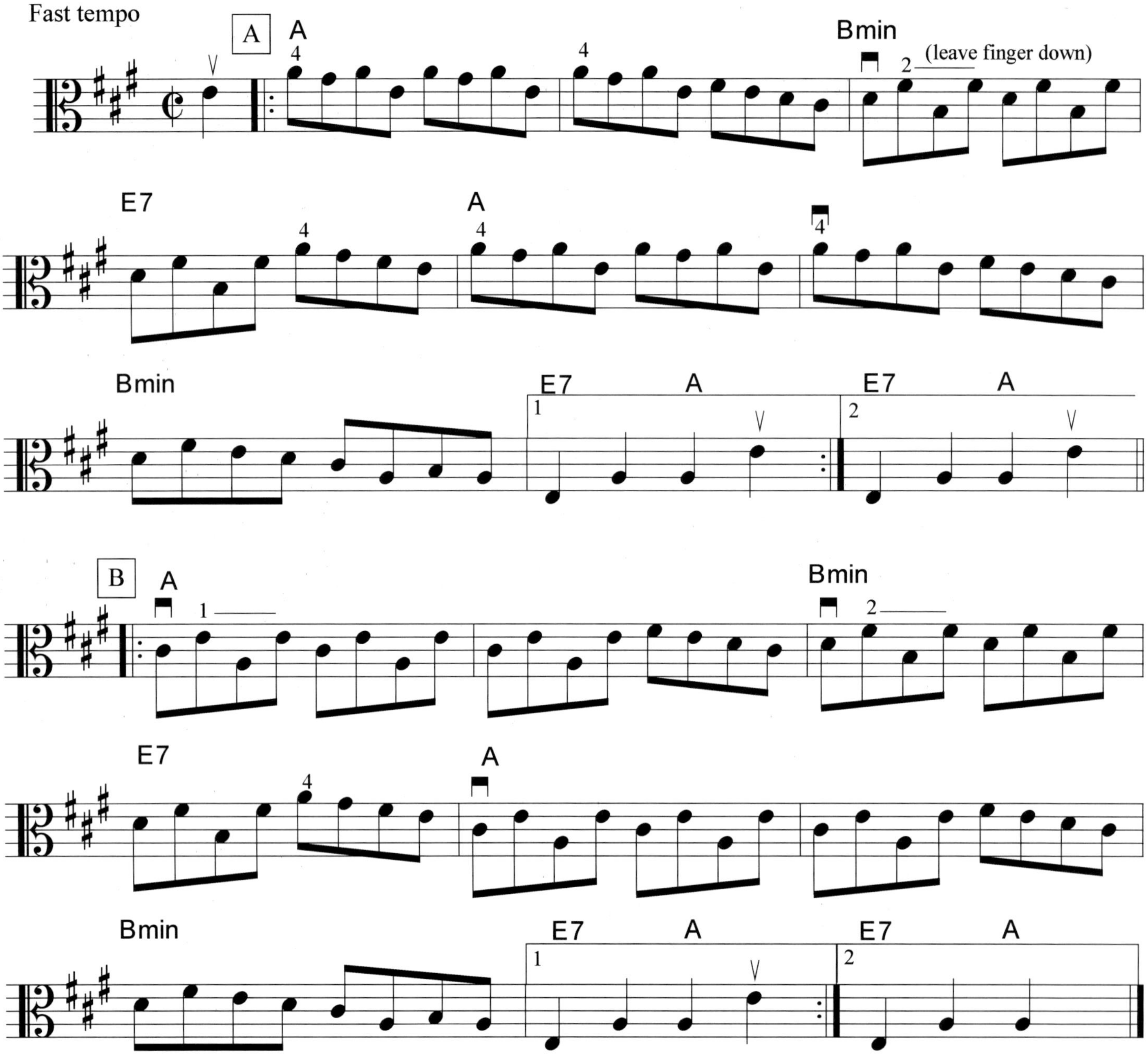

A
A 4 4 Bmin 2 (leave finger down)
E7 4 A 4 4
Bmin E7 A 1 E7 A 2

B
A 1 Bmin 2
E7 4 A
Bmin E7 A 1 E7 A 2

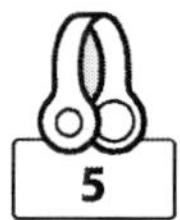

Devil's Dream

This version can be played in a medley with other tunes in the key of D.

Straight rhythm
Fast tempo

Traditional

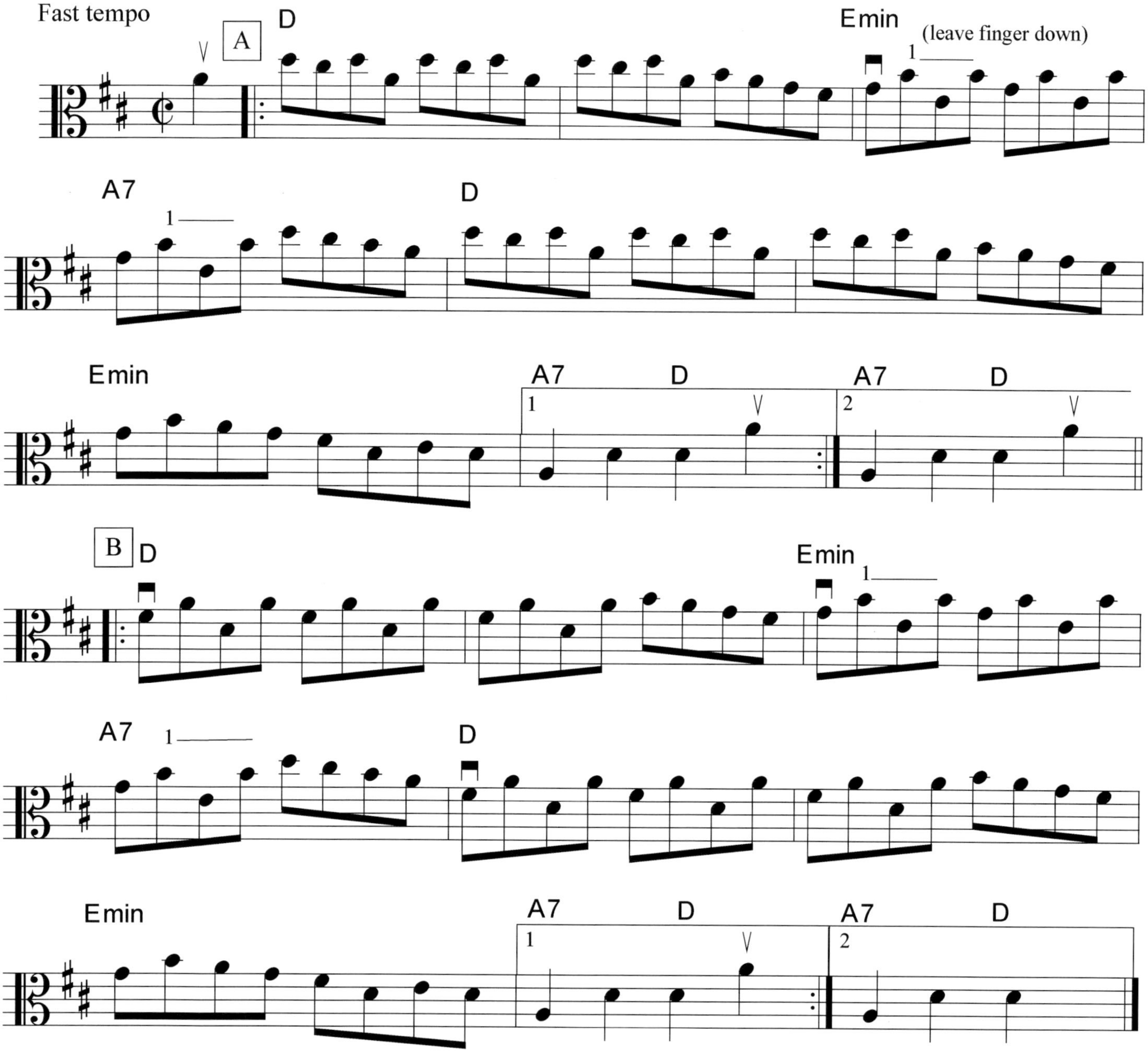

A
D
Emin
(leave finger down)
1
A7
1
D
Emin
A7
D
1
A7
D
2
B
D
Emin
1
A7
1
D
Emin
A7
D
1
A7
D
2

Staten Island

(Lower version)

In "Staten Island" you can use a more swingy rhythm on the eighth-note passages. This rhythm will give the tune a different feel than playing straight eighth notes.

Swing rhythm
Moderate tempo

Traditional

Staten Island

(Original version with shifting)

Swing rhythm
Moderate tempo

Traditional

Irish Washerwoman

Straight rhythm
Fast tempo

Traditional
Irish Jig

A
G D G D G G B G D C G C G D G G

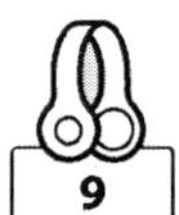

Garry Owen

This traditional tune could be played in a medley with "Irish Washerwoman". Slurs have been added for smoothness, but the tune could be played without slurs. "Garry Owen" is said to have been one of the songs played by a band as the 7th Cavalry headed out towards Little Big Horn. It was Custer's favorite battle tune.

Straight rhythm
Fast tempo

Traditional

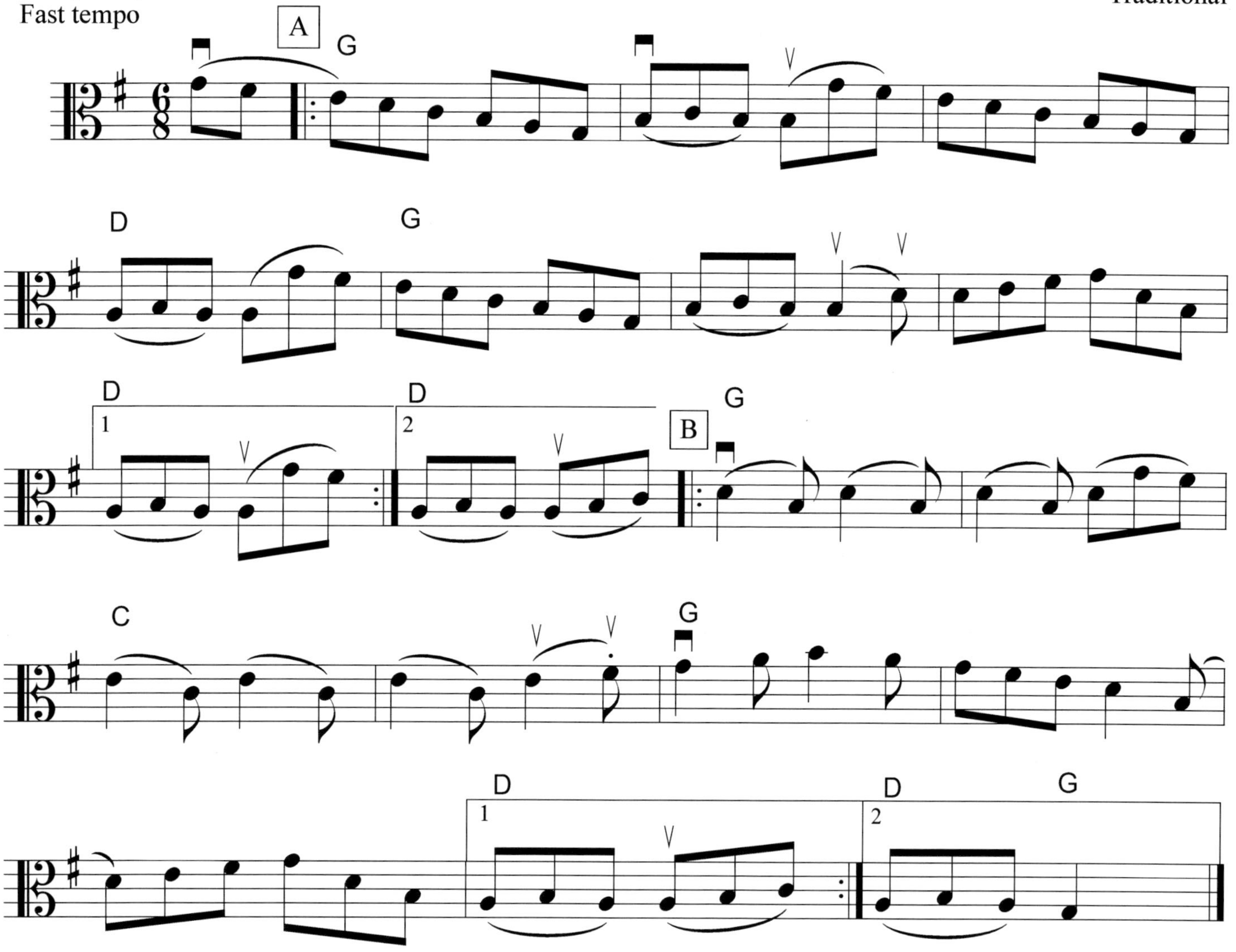

A G D G D D B G C G D D G

Red Haired Boy

Straight or swing rhythm
Moderate tempo

Traditional

In old-time fiddling each player has their own unique style, and you can hear different fiddlers play the same tune with many variations. Improvisation is an important part of the development of different styles. "Red Haired Boy" can be used as an example of how to change passages with simple improvistaion. To give the tune a more swingy feel, use a swing rhythm on all eighth-note passages.

Red Haired Boy

(Variation)

Straight or swing rhythm
Moderate tempo

Traditional

Both versions of "Red Haired Boy" could be played one after the other. This would add variety and interest to the tune if you are playing it through more than once.

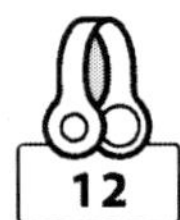

Wilson's Clog

(Simplified)

This version has been modified to play without shifting.
It is written here in 6/8 time to make the rhythm easier to read.

Traditional

Fast or moderate tempo

A

D G D

A7

D G D A7

E A7 D D

B

A7

D G D A7

E A7 D D

Wilson's Clog

(Lower, original version)

"Wilson's Clog" is also known as "Fred Wilson's Clog" or "Fred Wilson's Hornpipe".
It is written here in 6/8 time to make the rhythm easier to read.

Fast or moderate tempo

Traditional

A D G D

A7 4

D G D A7 4

E A7 D 1 D 2

B A7 1

D G D A7 4

E A7 D 1 D 2

Here's to the Ladies

This tune is also known as "To the Ladies".

Straight rhythm
Fast tempo

Traditional

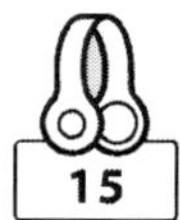

St. Anne's Reel

Swing rhythm
Fast or moderate tempo

Traditional

A D G A7 D G A7 D D B D Emin A7 D Emin A7 D D

Great Western Clog

This clog is also known as the "Great Western Lancashire Clog".
It has been written in 6/8 time to make the rhythm easier to read.

Moderate tempo

Traditional

A D A7 D A7 D A7 D D B G D A7 Emin G D A7 D A7 D D

C
D
A7
D
A7
D
A7
D
D

East Tennessee Blues

Swing rhythm
Fast or moderate tempo

Old-Time

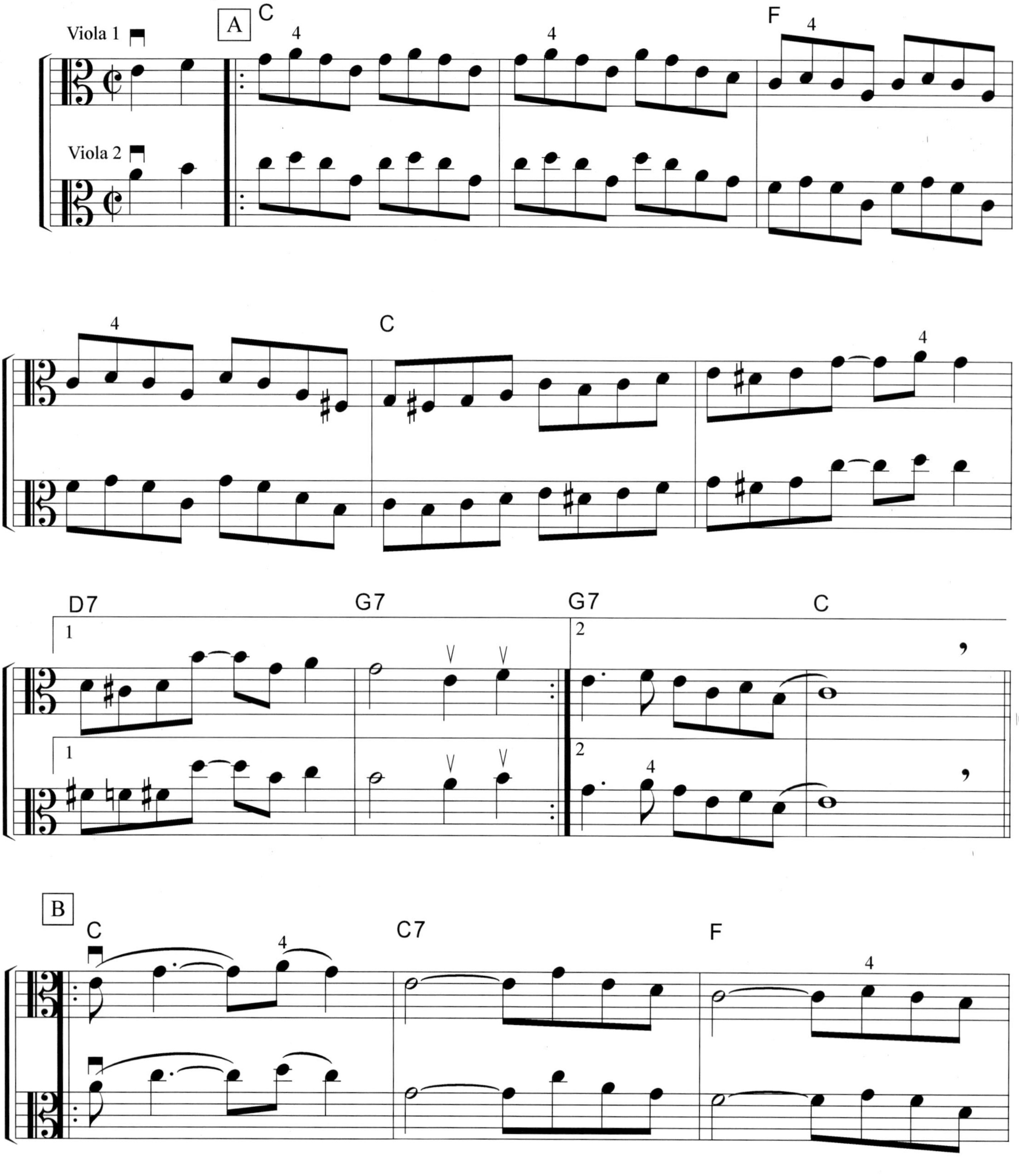

Viola 1
Viola 2

A

C F C D7 G7 G7 C

B

C C7 F

C
4
D7
G7
G7
C
1
2
1
2

My Silver Bell

Swing rhythm
Fast or moderate tempo

Old-time

A

Viola 1

Viola 2

G D7 G D7 G

D7 G

G D7 G D7 G

D7 G

B

G C

G
D7
G
G
C
G
D7
G

Whoa Mule

"Whoa Mule" uses finger slides to imitate the sound of a braying mule.
The symbol ⁄ means to slide your finger up to the note from one half step below.

Swing rhythm
Fast or moderate tempo

Attributed to
Tommy Jackson

A G C G C D7 G

C D7 G

B G C G C G C D7 G

G C G C G C D7 G

Fisher's Hornpipe

This version has been modified to play without shifting.

Straight or swing rhythm
Fast tempo

Traditional

A

D G D G

D G D A7 D G

D G D A7 D D

B A7 D A7

E A7 G D

G A7 D D

The B part using lower strings

B A7 D A7

E A7 G D

G A7 D D

Teetotaler's Reel

Straight rhythm
Fast or moderate tempo

This version has been modified to play without shifting.

Traditional

The A part with shifting.

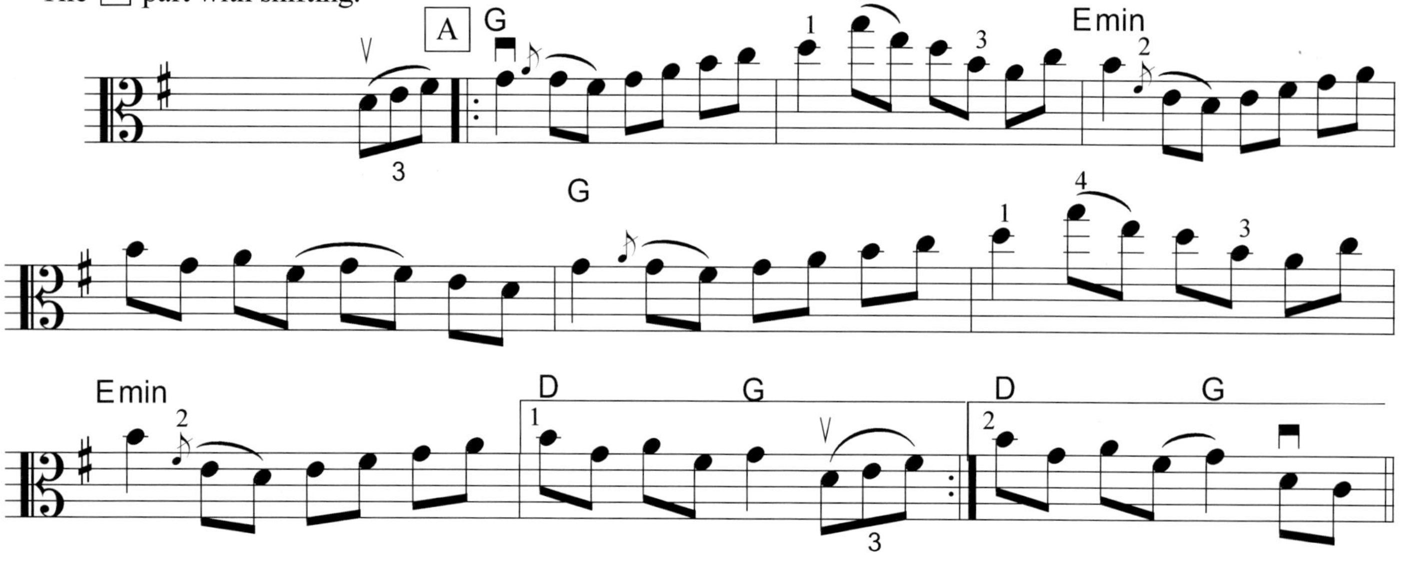

Temperance Reel

(Simplified)

The "Teetotaler's Reel" and "Temperance Reel" are two different versions of the same tune which is also known as "Kingsport" or "The Devil in Georgia". The two different versions can represent the contrast in styles of fiddling. "Temperance Reel" has some added variation to give it a different sound. Be sure to swing the rhythm. This version has been modified to play without shifting.

Swing rhythm
Fast or moderate tempo

Traditional

A

G Em

G

Em D G D G

B

Em D

Em

D G D G

Ragtime Annie

This version has been modified to play without shifting.

Straight rhythm
Fast or moderate tempo

Traditional

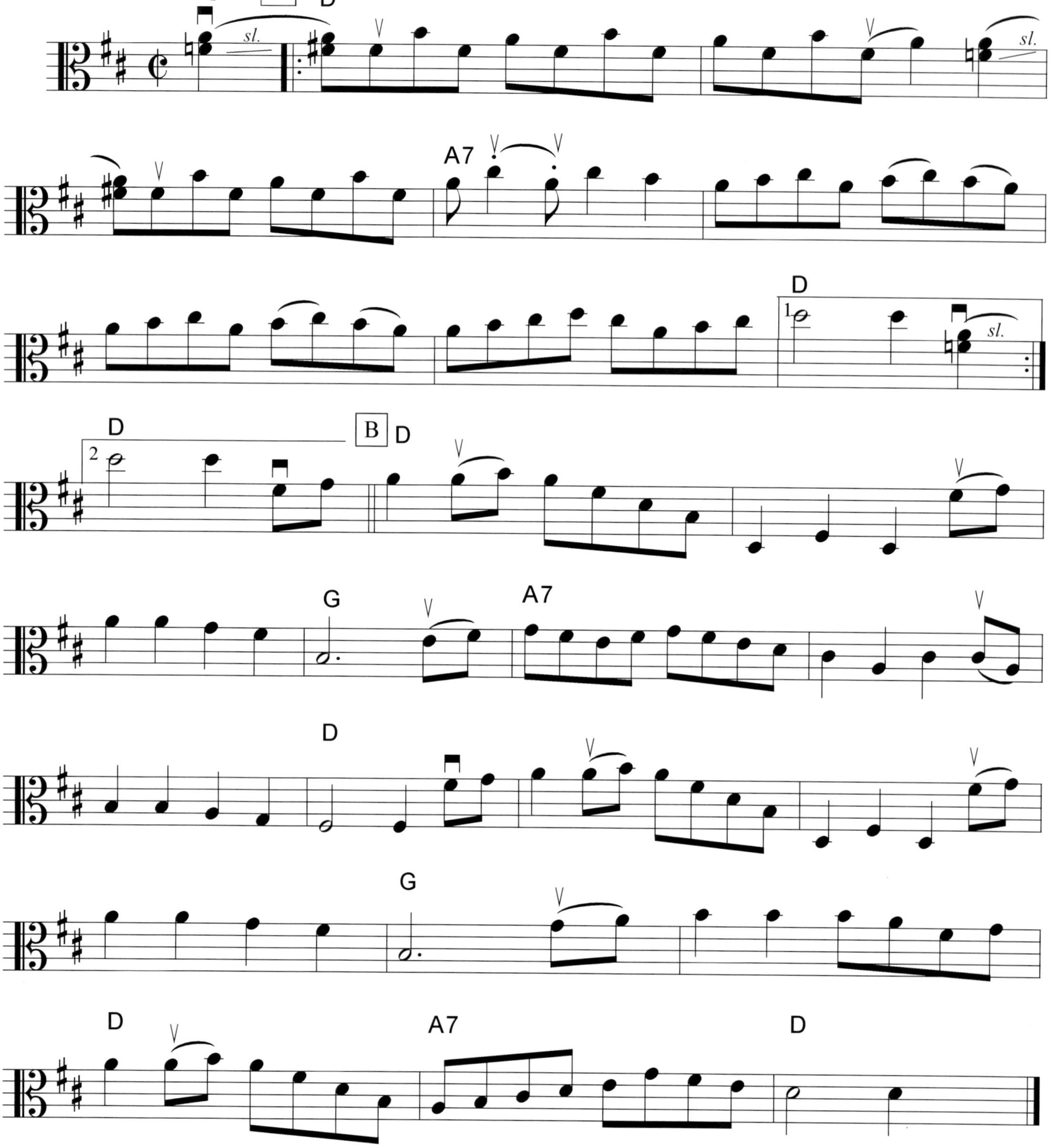

A D sl. A7 D sl. D B D G A7 D G D A7 D

Crazy Creek

"Crazy Creek", which has a very unique sound is best known as a bluegrass instrumental.

Swing rhythm
Fast or moderate tempo

Attributed to
Tommy Jackson

A D A D A D
(shift) A 2 C 1 (shift) 2
E A 1 A 2
B F C
F C E
A A D A D A D
A 2 C 1 2
E A

Benny & Bea's Waltz

(Simplified)

This version is modified to play without shifting.

Brenda Wallace
(Used by permission)

Swing rhythm on eighth notes
Danceable waltz tempo

Em C G

Em C Am

D Em C G

Em C D G

G 1 *Fine* G 2 Am D

G Em C D

G G Am D G

Em C D G *D.C. al Fine*

This waltz was written as a tribute to Benny Thomasson and his wife Bea.

26
Benny & Bea's Waltz
(Original version with shifting)
Brenda Wallace
(Used by permission)
Swing rhythm on eighth notes
Danceable waltz tempo
Em C G
Em C Am
D Em C G
Em C D G
G Fine G Am D
G Em C D
G G Am D G
Em C D G
D.C. al Fine

Goodnight Waltz

This version is modified to play without shifting. The guitar chords marked in parentheses are optional chords which can be added for more variety.

Swing rhythm on eighth notes
Danceable waltz tempo

Traditional

A C (B) C
G
G7 C
(B) C
C7 F (F♯dim) C
A7 Dm G7 C C7 *Fine*
B F E7 F
C7

The B section with shifting.

Angus Campbell

(Simplified)

Swing rhythm
Fast or moderate tempo

This version has been modified to play without shifting.

Traditional

Texas-Style Fiddling

Texas-style fiddling is a distinct style that brings elements of swing and jazz into traditional oldtime fiddle tunes. A player improvises passages of the tune to add variety. Players also listen to each other and mimic each other's playing. The style began in Texas with players such as Major Franklin, Lewis Franklin, Vernon Solomon, and Benny Thomasson. Benny Thomasson helped introduce the style to contests like the Weiser National Oldtime Fiddlers' Contest, and he taught many young fiddlers.

The following tunes are often played among Texas-style fiddlers and in fiddle contests. The versions are basic and have workable bowings.

Angus Campbell

(Lower, original version)

Swing rhythm
Fast or moderate tempo

Traditional

A A E7 A E7 A A
B A E7 A E7 A A

Bill Cheatum

(Simplified)

Swing rhythm
Fast or moderate tempo

Traditional

A D E7 A E7 A

B A D E7 A D A E7

A D E7 A D E7 A E7 A

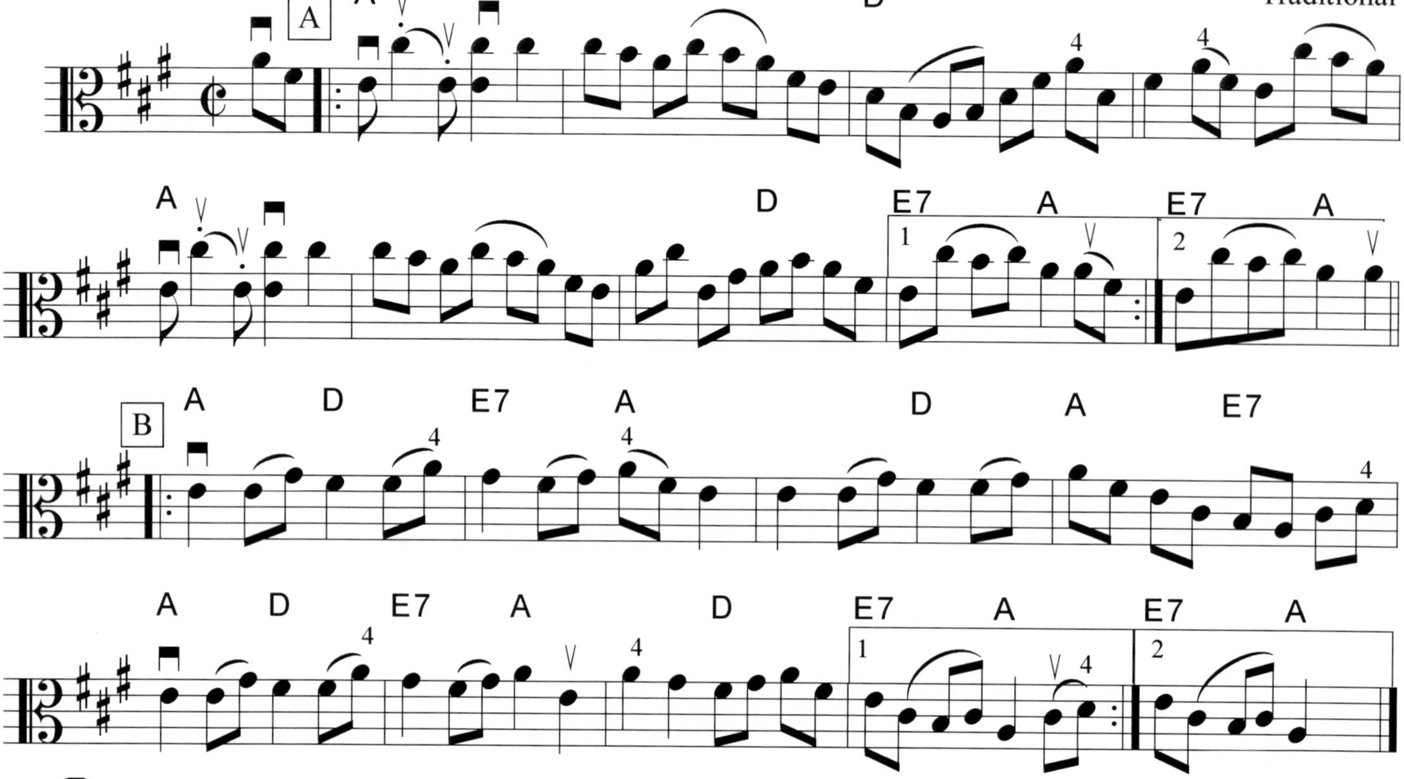

32

Bill Cheatum

(Original version, no shifting)

Swing rhythm
Fast or moderate tempo

Traditional

A D E7 A E7 A

B A D E7 A D A E7

A D E7 A D E7 A E7 A

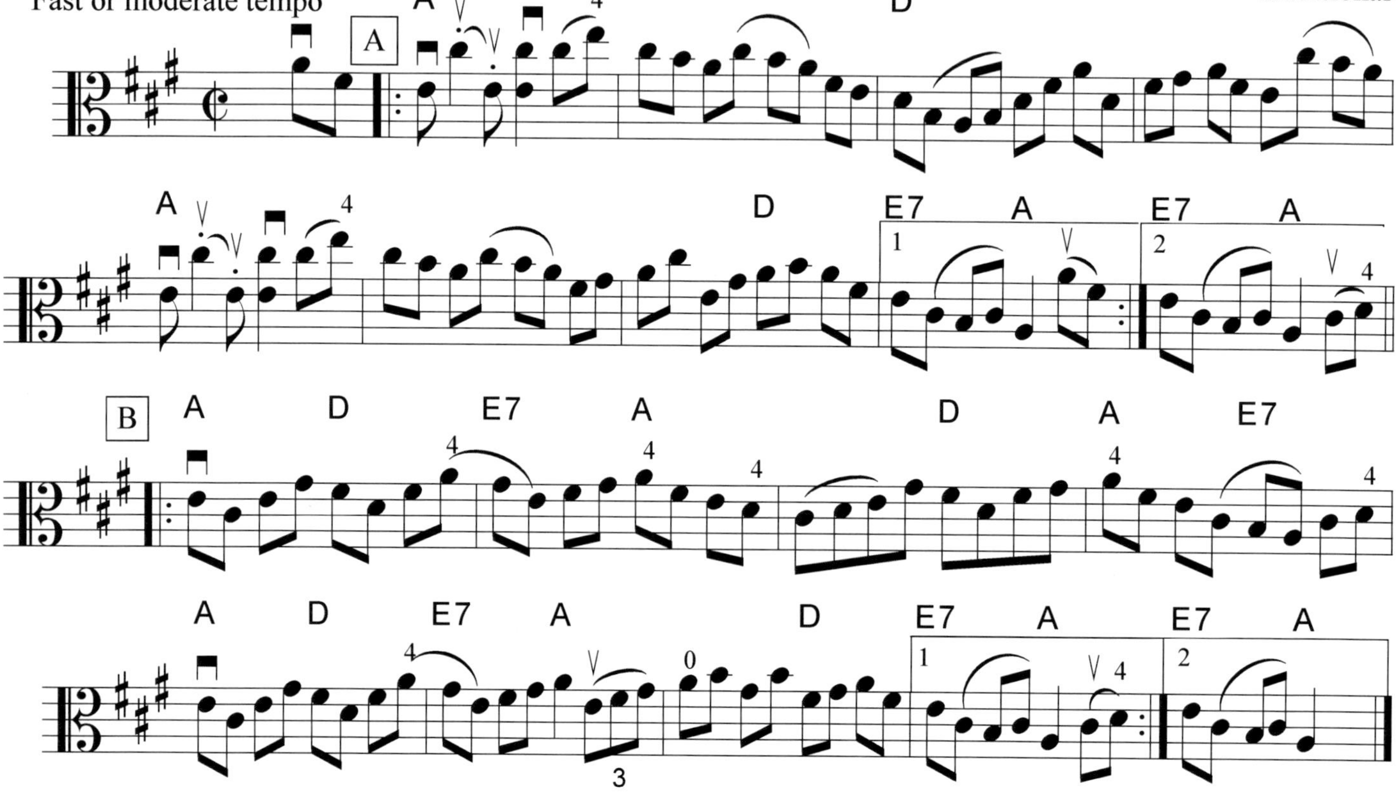

Forester's Reel

Swing rhythm
Fast or moderate tempo

Traditional

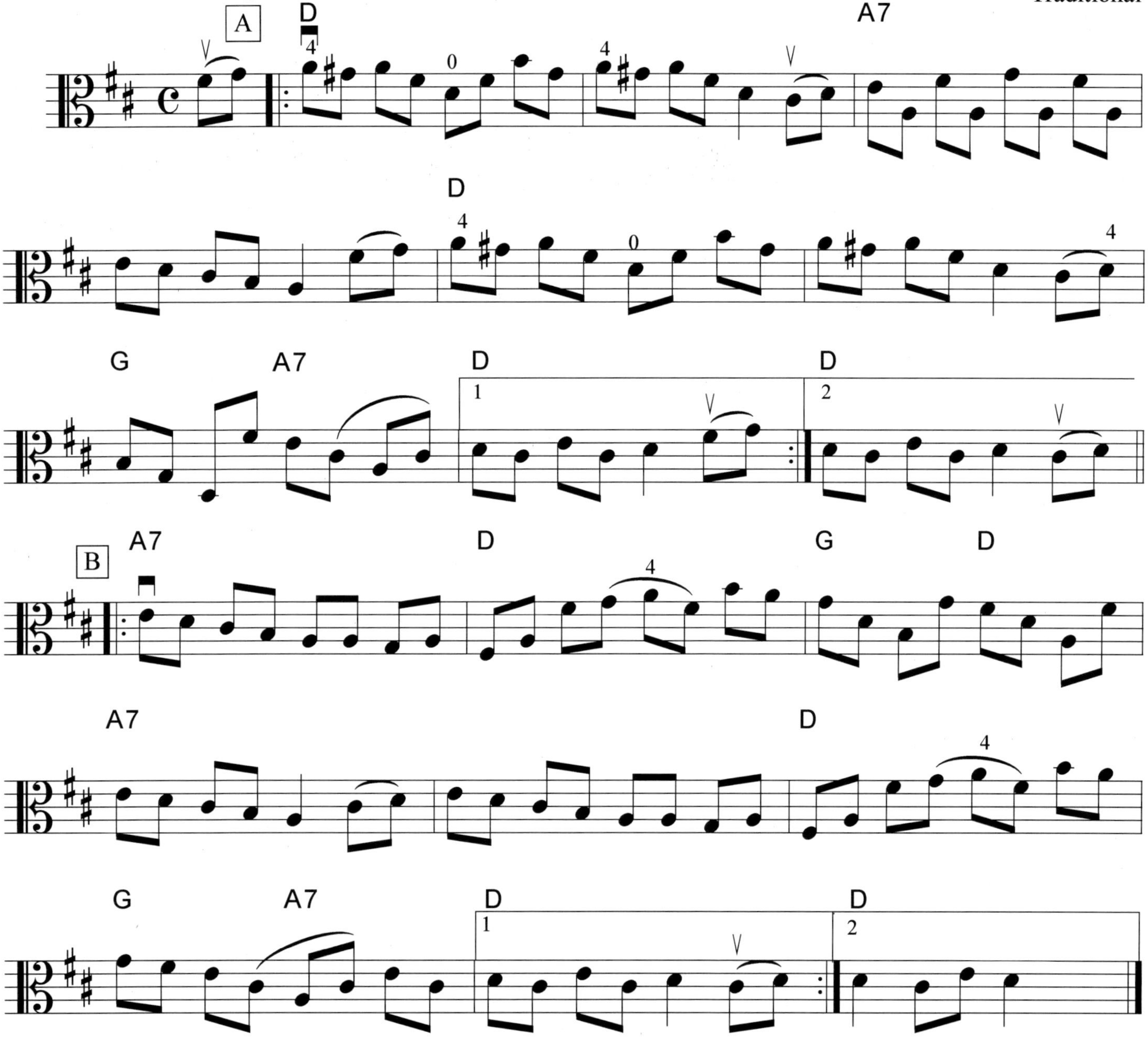

A

D A7

D

G A7 D D

B

A7 D G D

A7 D

G A7 D D

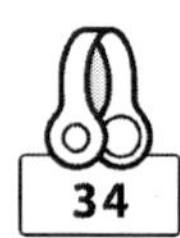

New Broom

Swing rhythm
Fast or moderate tempo

Traditional

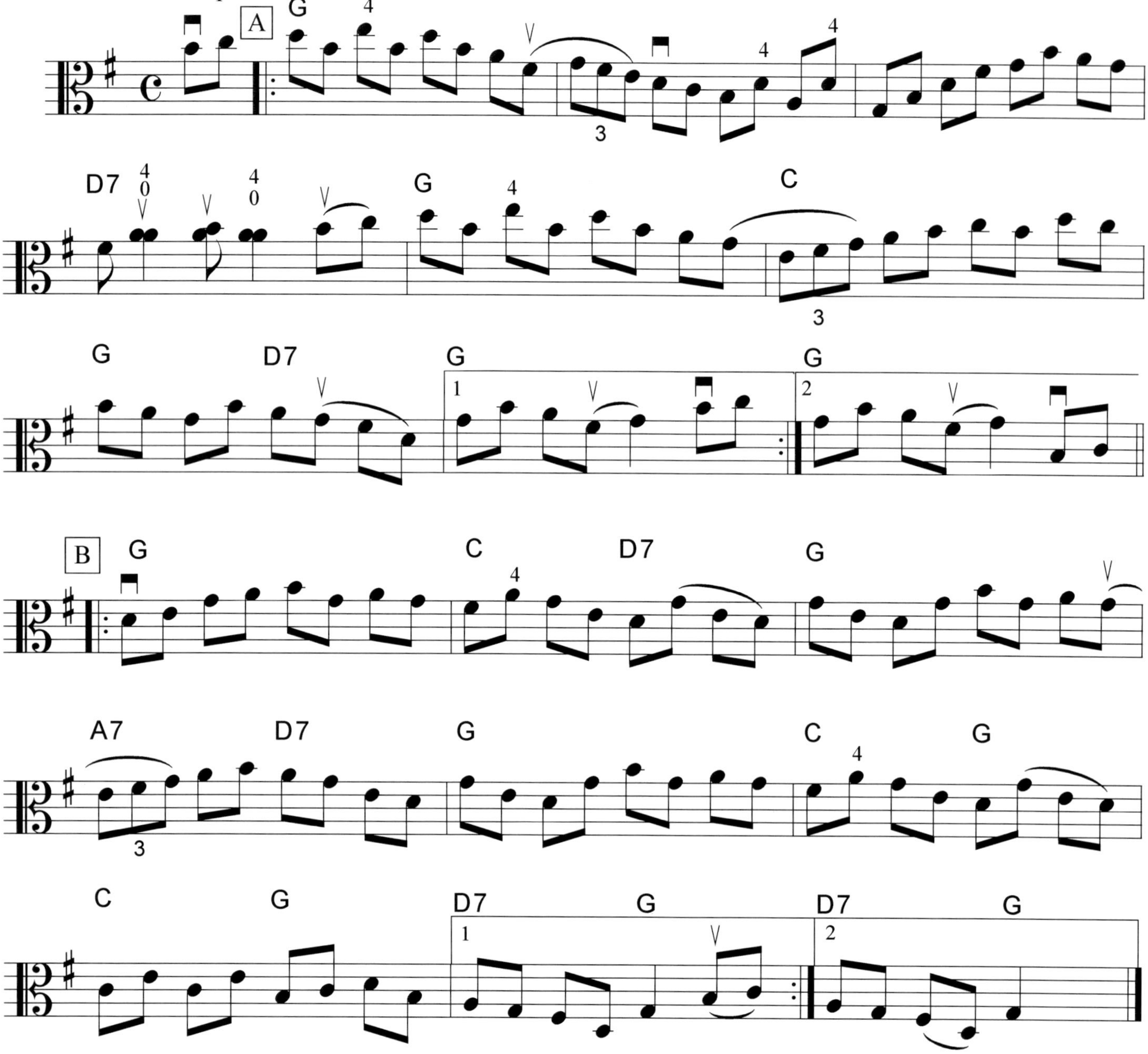

Snowflake Reel

This version has been modified to play without shifting.

Swing rhythm
Fast or moderate tempo

Attributed to
Wally Traugott

A D A7 D G A7 D 1 D 2 B D B♭ D A7 D 1 D 2

Cuckoo's Nest 1

(Simplified)

Several versions of Cuckoo's Nest are given here to show options for fingering and contrast in styles. This version has been modified to play without shifting.

Swing rhythm
Moderate tempo

Traditional

Cuckoo's Nest 1

37

(Original version with shifting)

Swing rhythm

Traditional

Cuckoo's Nest 2

(Simplified)

This version of Cuckoo's Nest shows how a tune can be played in different ways. This version uses more lower strings without shifting and slightly different noting patterns.

Swing rhythm
Moderate tempo

Traditional

39

Cuckoo's Nest 2

(Variation with shifting)

Traditional

Swing rhythm

Snowshoes

This version has been modified to play without shifting.

Swing rhythm
Fast or moderate tempo

Traditional

Forked Deer

This version has been modified to play without shifting.

Swing rhythm
Moderate tempo

Traditional

A D G D A7 D G D G A7 D A7 D B A D A7 D G A7 D A7 D

An open A string can be added as a double stop to the last measure of part A; double stops can also be added to the last three measures of part B as follows.

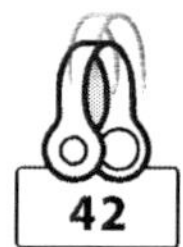

Swing rhythm
Fast or moderate tempo

Bittercreek

This version has been modified to be played without shifting.

Traditional

A G C G D7 G C G D7 G D7 G Fine B G C G D7 G C G D7 G D7 G C G C G D7 G C G D7 G D7 G

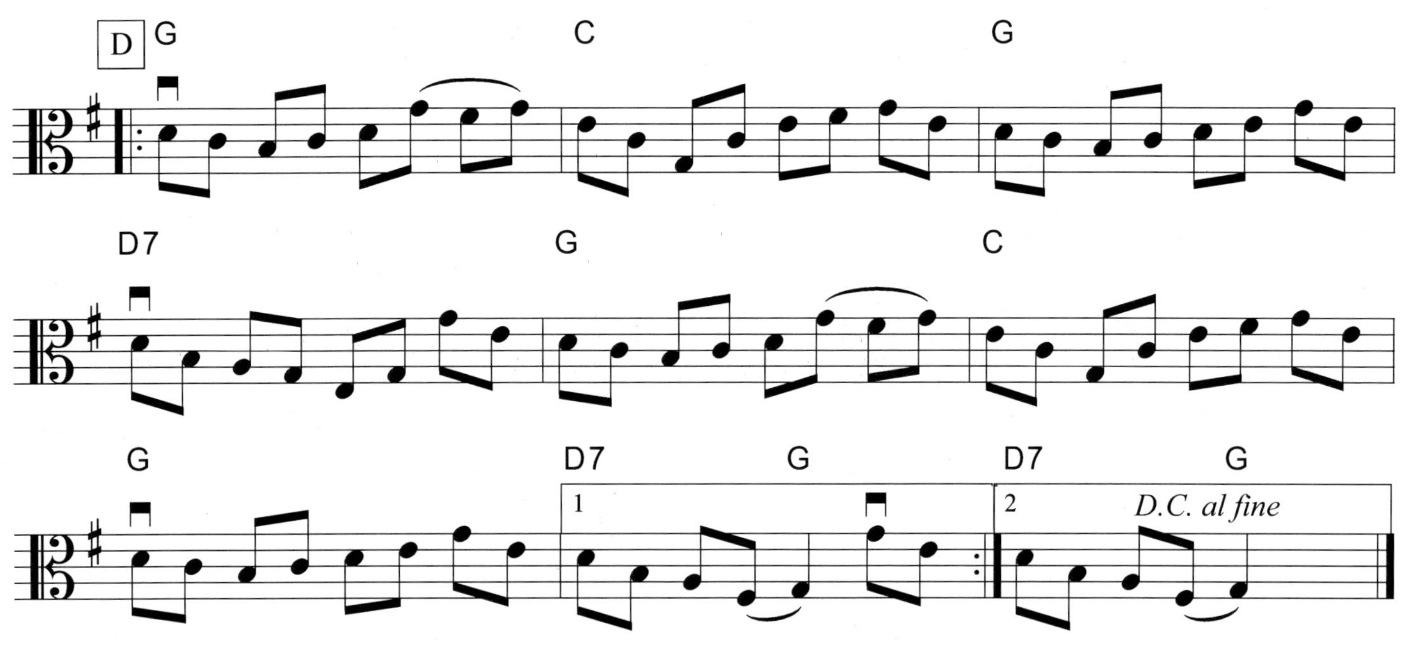
D
G
C
G
D7
G
C
G
D7
G
D7
G
1
2
D.C. al fine

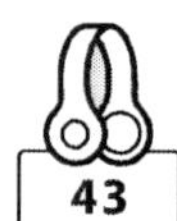

Salt River

This version has been modified to play without shifting.

Swing or straight rhythm

Traditional

This tune is popular among bluegrass musicians as "Salt Creek". In a bluegrass setting it should be played at a fast tempo and a straight rhythm. Played as a Texas-style hoedown, "Salt River" should have more of a swing rhythm and a moderate tempo.

Whiskey Before Breakfast

This version has been modified to play without shifting.

Swing rhythm
Fast or moderate tempo

Traditional

A D 0 4 G D 4 3
A7 D 0 4 3
G D A7 D 1 A7 D 2
B D Em 3
A7 D A7 G D 3 3
G D 4 A7 D 1 A7 D 2

Swing rhythm
Fast or moderate tempo

Cattle in the Cane

This version has been modified to play without shifting.

Traditional

Traditionally, the A and B parts of this tune would be reversed.

Black and White Rag

(Simplified)

This version has been modified to play without shifting.

Swing rhythm
Fast or moderate tempo

George Botsford

A E7 A E7 A E7 A F♯7 Bm E7 A 1 1 A Fine 2 B D B7 E7 A D

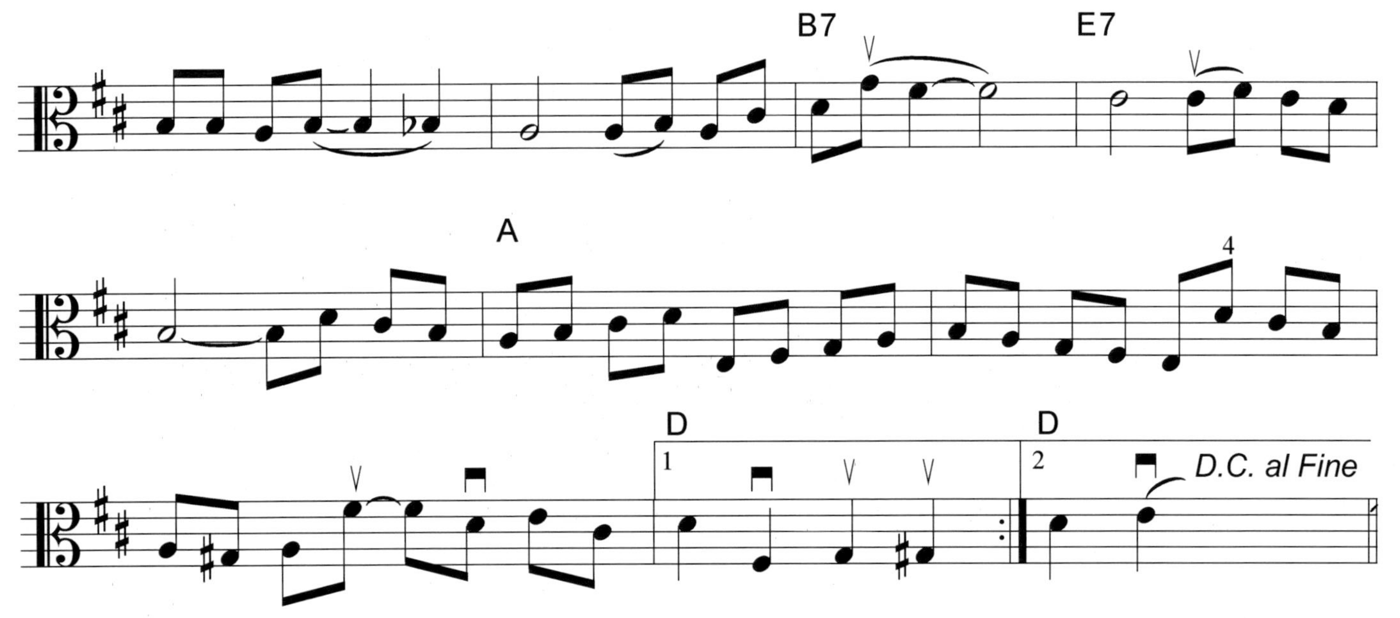
B7
E7
A
4
D
1
D
2
D.C. al Fine

Little Joe

This version has been modified to play without shifting.

Swing rhythm
Moderate tempo

A G D7 C G C G A D7 G D7 C G C G D7 G D7 G

B D A7 E7 A7 D A7 D D D7

C G C G A D7 G

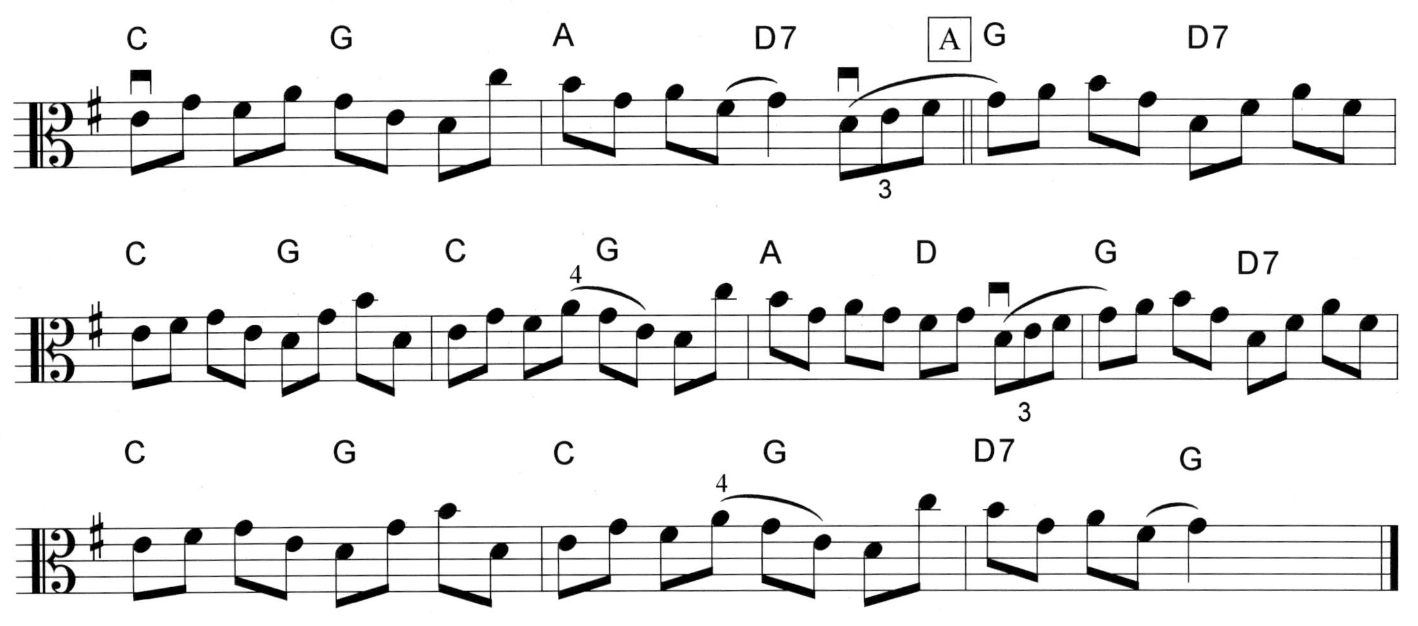
C G A D7 A G D7
3
C G C G A D G D7
4
3
C G C G D7 G
4

Other Mel Bay Viola Books

American Fiddle Tunes for Solo and Ensemble: Viola/Violin 3 (C. Duncan)
Modern Viola Method Grade 1 (Norgaard/Scott)
The American Fiddle Method for Viola Vol. 1 (Wicklund/Farr)
Celtic Fiddle Tunes for Solo and Ensemble: Viola/Violin 3 (C. Duncan)
Christmas Songs for Beginning Viola Level 1 (C. Duncan)
Christmas Strings: Viola/Violin 3 & Ensemble Score (Miller)
Classical Repertoire for Viola Vol. 1 (Puscoiu)
Easy Classics for Viola (Spitzer)
Easy Solos for Beginning Viola (C. Duncan)
Fiddling Classics for Solo & Ensemble: Viola/Violin 3 and Score (C. Duncan)
Fiddle Tunes for Two Violas (Phillips)
Fun with the Viola (W. Bay)
Hymns Made Easy for Viola (Clarke)
Jazz Viola Wizard Junior, Book 1 (Norgaard)
Jazz Viola Wizard Junior, Book 2 (Norgaard)
Music from Around the World for Solo & Ensemble: Viola/Violin 3 (Miller)
My Very Best Christmas: Viola (Khanagov)
Sacred Melodies for Solo Viola (C. Duncan)
Scottish Airs and Dances for Viola & Cello/or Solo Viola (Witt)
Scottish Fiddling for Viola (Witt)
Student's Book of Rounds: Viola (Worth)
The Student Violist: Bach (C. Duncan)
The Student Violist: Beethoven (C. Duncan)
The Student Violist: Handel (C. Duncan)
The Student Violist: Mozart (C. Duncan)
Wedding Music for Solo Viola (Curatolo)
Wedding Music for Violin and Viola (Staidle)
Beginner Viola Theory for Children Book 1 (M. Smith)
Beginner Viola Theory for Children Book 2 (M. Smith)
Beginner Viola Theory for Children Book 3 (M. Smith)
Speed Reading for Viola (Bauer)
Viola Wall Chart (Norgaard)
Warm-Ups for Violists Made Easy/Large Print Edition (Wheeler)

WWW.MELBAY.COM